MANIFESTOS FOR THE 21ST CENTURY

SERIES EDITORS: URSULA OWEN AND JUDITH VIDAL-HALL

Free expression is as high on the agenda as it has ever been, though not always for the happiest of reasons. Here, distinguished writers address the issue of censorship in a complex and fragile world where people with widely different cultural habits and beliefs are living in close proximity, where offence is easily taken, and where words, images and behaviour are coming under the closest scrutiny. These books will surprise, clarify and provoke in equal measure.

Index on Censorship is the only international magazine promoting and protecting free expression. A haven for the censored and silenced, it has built an impressive track record since it was founded 35 years ago, publishing some of the finest writers, sharpest analysts and foremost thinkers in the world. In this series with Seagull Books, the focus will be on questions of rights, liberties, tolerance, silencing, censorship and dissent.

UN peacekeepers search for bodies in the rubble after the earthquake in Haiti on 12 January 2010. Source: UNDP.

HUMANITARIAN
ASSISTANCE?
haiti and beyond

NEIL MIDDLETON

Seagull Books

LONDON NEW YORK CALCUTTA

Seagull Books 2010

ISBN-13 978 1 9064 9 776 7

British Library Cataloguing-in-Publication Data
A catalogue record for this book is available
from the British Library

Typeset and designed by Seagull Books, Calcutta, India
Printed at Graphic Prints, Calcutta

CONTENTS

Humanitarian assistance is offered to countries affected by disaster beyond their capacity to manage, or to countries whose states have collapsed, often as a result of prolonged internal warfare. In general, much popular support for humanitarian assistance rests on the assumption that it is disinterested and purely philanthropic. In practice, it is part of the international politics of those states wealthy enough to mount such programmes. Though poor countries are no longer directly colonized in the manner of the nineteenth and early twentieth centuries, they share, in one form or another, the problem of being incorporated into the donor's international policies and interests.

Yet the apparently ramshackle apparatus of humanitarian assistance is, within the limits imposed on it by donating governments, surprisingly effective. Its failures are usually a product either of under-funding or of people enmeshed in complex emergencies who are frequently put beyond aid by the belligerents. A recent example of the latter may be seen in Israel's war in Gaza. Others include the US–UK war in Afghanistan, the oil industry's proxy war in eastern Congo, China's support for tyrannical governments in both Sudan and Burma. But these are only the more widely reported of such events. Even in those humanitarian crises which are assisted, provision is commonly too little—in its 'Consolidated &

Flash Appeals' report of February 2010, ReliefWeb listed 14 countries for which it had made such appeals; only 15 per cent of the pledges had been fulfilled.

SETTING THE SCENE

That overseas development aid is largely an instrument in the industrialized world's exploitation of Third World resources is not a recent accusation. We have only to watch the international predators at work in controlling West Africa's recently exploited oil fields for an outstanding example. There are many others. The case is much the same in development's two-pronged cousin known as 'humanitarian assistance' and 'humanitarian intervention', which are the subject of this book.

Humanitarian assistance is, at governmental level, largely managed by ministries of defence and foreign affairs. 'Assistance' means the delivery of a wide range of goods, services and personnel to sustain and protect people afflicted by disaster and whose governments either cannot meet their needs or have been destroyed. The latter are usually referred to as 'failed states' and Somalia is one prominent instance. 'Interventions' may include some or all of the elements of assistance, but activities in the field are often led by armed forces, some of which are managed by the UN, others by NATO, the EU or, to a lesser degree, the African Union (AU). The use of such forces is necessary because they are often the only organizations with the equipment and personnel capable of meeting the need.

Humanitarian disasters (or 'emergencies') are events which lead to substantial losses of human lives, livelihoods, homes and security. For the purposes of analysis—a necessary preliminary to offering assistance to those in need—they are divided into two categories: complex emergencies and natural disasters.[1] 'Complex' is the adjective given to disasters caused by human violence and well-known examples include, among several others, the wars against Vietnam, Iraq and the Palestinians, and the turmoil in Somalia, Sudan and eastern Congo. 'Natural' indicates large-scale destruction caused by natural events, of which the 2004 tsunami in the Indian Ocean is a major instance. So too was the earthquake in Haiti which began on 12 January 2010 and was followed by at least 52 aftershocks within the following two weeks. The distinction between 'complex' and 'natural' is no more than a rough guide—since either can merge into the other—but the responses to each differ.

Assistance usually involves the transfer of goods (particularly food), personnel and some finance, and is generally given by relatively wealthy states to countries which, for whatever reason, are unable to deal adequately with an emergency without that help. Funds are generated from governments, non-governmental organizations (NGOs) and public donations. Frontline personnel are usually an uneasy mix of UN specialists and members of international non-governmental organizations (INGOs). Something like this sketchy account of what is, in practice, a far more complicated and profoundly political phenomenon is—when they think about it at all—how many people understand the overall mechanism. But popular understanding of how it all works lags well behind a far greater public interest in the reported events on the ground and the often heroic efforts of both the victims of calamity and of the humanitarians bringing relief. The problems raised by such enthusiasm may be seen in the piecemeal responses to disaster in general—effective aid is often only apparent in the disasters that catch the attention of the news media. Haiti is just such a case, in which the inevitable chaos in bringing relief was more immediately visible to the world.

Humanitarian aid is usually coordinated by the UN and comes from a variety of sources or blocs. One is the Western bloc, comprising North American, European and some antipodean and Latin American states. Others—each of them separate—are an alliance of some Muslim states, the Russian Federation, China, India and Japan (the latter sometimes joins the Western bloc). These blocs usually come together only in the sense that each of them contributes to the UN in general and in particular to its two major funding mechanisms for humanitarian assistance: the Consolidated Appeal Process (CAP) and the Central Emergency Response Fund (CERF). This book is primarily concerned with the Western bloc which funds humanitarian assistance largely in the ways in which its populations understand the term. Other blocs or sources usually, though not always, confine themselves to infrastructure and investment.[2]

The principal funders and organizers of humanitarian aid fall into distinct political camps. One may be called the internationalist group which primarily consists of the UN and the Red Cross/Red Crescent family; the other is largely made up of national governments and corporate and individual donors. It is important always to examine with care the motives and demands made by members of NGOs who insist that politics have no place in humanitarian action. At the least, when not expounding their own (political) agenda, they tend to confuse the distinction between politics and their necessary subset—political parties.

Complex emergencies are frequently long-term events, lasting often for years. Sporadic and apparently random irruptions of armed violence recur, commonly resulting in the withdrawal of front-line assistance and the destruction of any progress that has been made towards achieving some sort of safety and normality. Somalia and Sudan, both of which I was able to visit, are prime examples and will be considered at greater length in due course. Popular funding for complex emergencies is far more limited than for natural disasters. Many UN organizations, INGOs and varying parts of the Red Cross family make heroic efforts to help, but they are rarely sufficient, either in numbers or resources, to meet what are often gigantic needs.

Natural disasters can attract considerable public sympathy and substantial popular funding coupled with a natural desire for all such funds to be applied to front-line activities—shelter, food, water, medical attention and so on. There is little public recognition of the need for adequately funded systems of organization, acquisition, transport, delivery and the need for long-term support. For example, droughts, floods, earthquakes and epidemics kill people and their livestock, destroy livelihoods and cause massive displacement and conflict. In 10 years' time, Haiti will probably prove to be an outstanding illustration of this short-term thinking.

THE EMERGENCE OF HUMANITARIANISM

Wars are on every hand—the greatest of them are waged by forces available to powerful politicians against people whose only defence seems to be guerrilla activity. Wars aside, predatory attacks by international finance capital on the hard-won gains of working people in the developed world are common and are pursued with even greater ruthlessness in exploiting workers in poverty-stricken Third World states. Economic interventions have amounted to rapine; War on Want has pointed out that the UK's biggest overseas development quango, the Commonwealth Development Corporation (CDC, a development finance organization owned by the UK's Department for International Development), 'uses private equity-type policies' which include 'the use of offshore tax havens, to exploit local businesses and to avoid paying tax to hard-pressed governments'.[3]

The home states of international capital have invented humanitarian assistance as one palliative tool among others—one in which foreign policy sanctions sticking plaster for major wounds.[4] One of the first and most constant lines of humanitarian assistance is for refugees, particularly those fleeing from war or other violence. Despite their growing numbers, they are still a minority among those driven from their homes. Many more people are also forced to move, although they do not leave their countries—they are commonly described as 'internally displaced persons' (IDPs). Statistics for the latter are hard to come by, not least because many of them manage to survive by their own efforts, are anxious not to be identified and prefer, wherever possible, to be absorbed into the community to which they have fled. Others are housed in dubious camps, often established with foreign aid. But they are camps and generally not prisons—so the number of people in them changes constantly. Yet others, particularly those who are nomadic pastoralists, try to create their own places of safety where they can look after those animals that still remain.

In various ways, the United Nations Refugee Agency (UNHCR) assists what it calls 'people of concern'. At the time of writing, its most up-to-date figures for refugees throughout the world were for 2007 and amounted to 11,390,600—an increase over the preceding two years by almost 25 per cent. Of these, between 83 and 90 per cent stay close to the borders of their countries, leaving the rest of the world to cope with a little over 1 million people. Government hysteria has led to a refusal to accept the UNHCR's recognition of people forced from their own countries as refugees and to an insistence on classifying, almost branding, most of them as 'asylum-seekers', a status that can last for years. Some of them may, following extra-judicial inquiries, be accorded the status of refugees. The UN's Universal Declaration of Human Rights uses the expression literally: it refers to people who are asking for refuge—asking to be recognized as refugees. But in many wealthy countries, particularly the UK, Ireland and Denmark, 'asylum-seeker' has become a term of opprobrium. The governments of each of these countries have persuaded their citizens that asylum-seekers are dangerously dubious characters who must be contained, controlled and, as far as possible, prevented from settling.

humanitarian assistance?

HOW MANY REFUGEES AND WHERE ARE THEY FROM?

UNHCR REGIONS	REFUGEES	PEOPLE IN REFUGEE-LIKE SITUATIONS*	TOTAL REFUGEES (LATE 2007)
Central Africa & Great Lakes	1,100,100	-	1,100,100
East and Horn of Africa	815,200	-	815,200
Southern Africa	181,200	-	181,200
West Africa	174,700	-	174,700
Americas	499,900	487,600	987,500
Asia and Pacific	2,675,900	1,149,100	3,825,000
Europe	180,200	5,100	1,585,300
Middle East & North Africa	2,654,000	67,600	2,721,600
TOTALS	9,681,200	1,709,400	11,390,600

*'Refugee-like situations' is a UNHCR category 'of persons [. . .] outside their country or [. . .] territory of origin and who face protection risks similar to those of refugees, but for whom refugee status has [. . .] not been ascertained' (UNHCR.org).

Complex emergencies—major causes of refugeedom—are obviously political events; they are certainly caused by them, but their management and relief are also integral parts of international political manoeuvre. In order to understand the dynamic of politicized humanitarianism, it is necessary, first, to look at the ideological origins of its structures. In Europe, early moves towards assistance for those afflicted by war arose from the treatment of injured soldiers. But contemporary practice emerged from the foundation, by Jean-Henri Dunant, of the Red Cross movement and its subsequent international development into the Red Cross/Red Crescent family which insists on impartiality. Following the end of the First World War, the formulation in his 'Fourteen Points' of a new world order by US President Woodrow Wilson led to the recognition of assistance as a necessary part of a government's foreign policies.[5]

Dunant successfully campaigned for the establishment of an international treaty which recognized the special position of his movement. Entitled the 'Convention for the Amelioration of the Wounded in Time of War', it referred directly to the protection of wounded soldiers. Concluded in Geneva in 1864, it became the first of four treaties and two protocols, now known collectively as the 'Geneva Conventions'; the last protocol was agreed upon in 1949.[6] International recognition of the role of the Red Cross in the development and establishment of these treaties led to the organization's not unreasonable claim to be the 'guardian of international humanitarian law'. But what it cannot do is enforce it, nor can it always evade compromising concessions. The limitations of that guardianship are clear, and two examples will illustrate the point. Ilan Pappe remarks on one of the most famous and extreme instances of limitations on Red

Cross activity—during the Nazi regime, the Red Cross visited concentration camps, but did not report on what went on in them.[7] The second example is more recent—from 2002, the Red Cross frequently visited Guantánamo Bay, but the US government allowed it to do so only on the condition that it did not report on the abuses taking place in that prison.[8]

During the Russo-Turkish war of 1876, the Ottoman Empire adopted the symbol of the Red Crescent for medical assistance on the battlefield. The first Geneva Convention recognized it as having the same status as the symbol of the Red Cross and the International Federation of the Red Cross (IFRC) adopted it—thus the initials 'RC' came to mean both 'Red Cross' and 'Red Crescent' and, most recently, Israel's 'Red Crystal'. At the Twentieth International Conference of the Red Cross and Red Crescent, held in Vienna in 1965, the movement proclaimed its seven Fundamental Principles: humanity, impartiality, neutrality, independence, voluntary service, unity and universality. For the purposes of this discussion, the second of these—impartiality—is of the greatest interest. But, before returning to it, we should consider the other political aspect of humanitarian assistance—the fact that it is part of foreign policy.

Wilson's importance lies in his recognition of humanitarian interventions as constituents of foreign policy and his consequent cavalier use of them, or at least of their language, in advancing such policy aims. But he merely formulated the practice; its origins lie further back in the history of the US. Early in the twentieth century, President William H. Taft made a populist speech in which he predicted a time when the nation's flag would fly at equidistant points from the North to the South Poles marking the territory which is 'ours', a claim he held to be justified by the racial superiority of the people of the US.[9] Eduardo Galeano describes the murderous activities of the adventurer William Walker, who, in the mid-nineteenth century, operated in Latin America in the interests of the Morgan and Garrison Bank. His filibustering took place in Nicaragua, El Salvador and Honduras—he appointed himself President of Nicaragua, restored slavery wherever he held sway and became a national hero in the US.[10] In the Pacific, the Philippines had declared its independence from Spain in 1896, but at the end of the US–Spanish war in 1898, Spain ceded its claim on the islands to the US. In the first 12 of years US occupation, over 500,000 Filipinos were killed in their renewed fight for independence. Among them were the 900 women, children and men—none of them combatants—slaughtered by US troops in the infamous Moro Massacre of March 1906.[11]

Wilson's own bloody contribution to expansion was in the same tradition. During his presidency, which ran for two terms from 1913 to 1921, he either began or continued the US military occupations of Mexico, Haiti, Santo Domingo, Cuba and Nicaragua. Most, if not all, of these events were represented to the US public and to the rest of the world as humanitarian interventions. Nineteenth- and early-twentieth-century European empires (particularly the British) had commonly excused their depredations and violence by claiming that the 'natives' were backward and needed the discipline and protection that only an 'advanced' civilization could provide. Territorial expansion, the consequent acquisition of resources and the politico-military dominance it both indicated and strengthened, were all achieved in the name of humanitarianism. Wilson's expansion of US imperialism in the twentieth century followed suit.

Wilsonian imperial campaigns established a new element in what is referred to in the jargon as the 'delivery' of assistance—the deployment of the benefactors' army in the process. Others who have also presented their operations as humanitarian protection, particularly in Africa since the end of the Second World War, have adopted the US stance.[12] In contemporary practice, the use of military forces is justified by claims that no other organizations have the flexibility and logistical skills necessary for the purpose. It is probably true that relatively successful assistance only became possible once troops had been deployed in the case of major disasters such as the tsunami of 2004 that caused such havoc in most of the countries along the seaboard of the Indian Ocean or the Haiti earthquake of 2010.

In the tsunami region, the forces of the US Pacific Command are more or less permanent features and were able to land their troops in Indonesia quite rapidly. The White House claimed that by February 2005, just over four weeks after the event, 16,000 troops were engaged in relief work.[13] But 'relief' came at a price. On 17 January, the erstwhile US Defense Secretary Paul Wolfowitz was recommending the sale of arms by the US to Indonesia even though such sales had previously been banned because of Indonesian oppression in Aceh and East Timor. He went on to suggest that military ties between the two countries should be strengthened and that talks should begin between Admiral Fargo, Commander of the US Pacific Command and the Indonesian chief of the military, General Endriartono Sutarto.[14] All this is in the interests of the US' strategies in the Pacific and is a good example of the use of humanitarian assistance as a bargaining chip.

Forces other than those deployed around the world by the US are also engaged in emergency assistance and with varying degrees of success. One example of a deeply troubled military presence in a humanitarian crisis is that of the forces of the African Union in Darfur. If an external agency was in any way to succeed in bringing an end to or moderating that crisis, then the AU was, and is, the most appropriate. This was a proposition apparently backed and financially supported by the wealthy nations of the world. Although such promises are often designed to satisfy the demands of the donors' own people and are quietly forgotten once attention has wavered. When I visited Darfur in 2005, AU soldiers were few, unpaid and without adequate supplies. Shortly before relinquishing the presidency in 2009, George W. Bush and his accomplices agreed to a joint UN–AU force for protection in the region. Since the UN is to lead this initiative and since the force is subject to the Security

Council, it gives the powerful nations more purchase in Sudan. Given the disparate interests in the region of the Council's members, it is by no means clear that such purchase will be benign.

Humanitarian assistance in complex emergencies, particularly when they reach the chronic stage, calls for large-scale and continuous funding which can only be met by coalitions of wealthy states. Funds, parts of which are frequently in kind, are delivered either multilaterally through the UN and the Red Cross/Red Crescent group, or bilaterally through the multiple agencies, principally NGOs, operating in the field. The two systems usually act in tandem and often overlap. With some obvious exceptions, such as Iraq, Afghanistan and Palestine, contemporary assistance tends not to be so blatantly imperialist as in the past, but it does remain attached to the donor nations' foreign policies and is used to further their diplomatic and, ultimately, economic ends. In many cases, both humanitarian and development assistance are managed by state ministries; the United States Agency for International Development (USAID), for example, is active in delivering assistance and is a part of the US Department of State. The irresoluble point of contradiction in humanitarian assistance as an element in foreign policy clearly lies in the complexity of relations between the global financial interests of powerful nations and corporations and the countries and regions particularly susceptible to complex disaster.

The crude machinations of the powerful in the Middle East provide a simple example. However, as battles for resources and control are inescapably related to economies and politics—both domestic and international—there are few, if any, instances of humanitarian assistance unaffected by them. Many complex emergencies, if not all, have at their roots the ambitions of the more powerful nations. Among the more obvious examples are the wars in Iraq, Afghanistan and the Caucasus.

'Impartiality' is the principle that most obviously distinguishes the Red Cross position from the 'political assessment' of the Wilsonian camp since, as Brian Barry points out, it comes in more than one kind. In his work *Justice as Impartiality* (1995), Barry distinguishes three issues: 'The Common-sense Idea of Impartiality', the 'Impartial Conceptions of the Good' and 'Consequentialist Impartiality.'[15] For our purposes, the second of these is of the greatest interest, but each of them calls for specific forms of behaviour, which means, in Barry's words 'that impartiality is not a strong organizing concept within common-sense morality [. . .] it is not a primary notion generating subsidiary ones'.[16] This is because in any case in which the issue arises, it is necessary to identify the reasons for insisting on impartiality. Obviously enough, impartiality in humanitarian assistance in complex emergencies is conditioned by the donor's perception of what would be good for the sufferers. Agreement about what constitutes the good is sparse, but, even if such an agreement were reached, the appropriate means of achieving it remains a matter of dispute. Barry suggests that we must 'anticipate that the normal state of affairs will be one in which there is no consensus on the nature of the good'.[17]

This dilemma has led INGOs into the formulation of what they tend to call 'a rights-based agenda' in the administration of both development and humanitarian assistance. These agendas look at rights abuses in, and largely by, poor countries, but fail to look at the abuses of economic rights in the development programmes of their own countries.[18]

A curious elision takes place in much NGO anti-poverty rhetoric. 'Market' is a term used with astonishing profligacy to include, without much distinction, the street-food vendors in Nairobi, for example, as well as the extortion by corporations of staggering copyright and patent fees for transferred technology.[19] Development becomes a mix of several conditions, including the improvement of agriculture, infrastructure, education, processing for raw materials and the possibility of selling finished products (rather than raw materials) in the markets of the developed world. What this, and many similar accounts of paths to development, conceals is that the process is directed at incorporating the poor into the very system which is the principal cause of their existing misery. In short, the NGO rights-based approach generally fails to consider what pursuing the right to development or to humanitarian assistance at present entails. Few of their programmes for either, whether rights-based or otherwise, do more than apply sticking plaster to life-threatening injuries—a situation which will continue until NGOs recognize that the states that fund them are frequently complicit with the corporations in creating the problems they attempt to solve. These points are illustrated by two long-standing complex disasters—Somalia and Sudan. But first, the most devastating recent instance of a natural disaster—Haiti 2010.

12 JANUARY 2010: EARTHQUAKE IN HAITI

It can come as no surprise that poorer countries, particularly those in geologically unstable regions, are prone to disaster. Earthquakes are not confined to poor countries—for example, in the late twentieth century, Italy was afflicted by three such catastrophes[20]—but the difference lies in the extent of the state's ability to both reduce risks by sophisticated planning, construction and organization and have in place adequate emergency provision. Wealthy states can also employ risk-reducing technologies, including the design and construction of buildings, and determine where and what should be built. The poor have few such protective measures.

With a population of about 9 million, Haiti is among the 20 poorest countries in the world and is one of the most environmentally devastated. Since the country lies on a fault line between the Caribbean and the North American tectonic plates, that poverty is massively exacerbated by the geology of the region. The recent earthquake, which began on 12 January 2010, was particularly disastrous—best estimates suggest that at least 230,000 people were killed, 300,000 were injured and 1 million were rendered homeless. In addition to the human casualties, Haitian government estimates suggest that 250,000 homes and 30,000 workplaces and shops were either destroyed or badly damaged. Casualties on this scale were a consequence of poverty, which, in turn, springs from a history of colonization, both direct and indirect, and of a subsequent neo-colonization which continues to this day. Other states are also afflicted by natural calamities but have prepared for them and, where possible, built defences—Chile, struck by an even more powerful earthquake less than two months after Haiti, is a good example. In order to make sense of the apparently disproportionate horrors visited on Haiti, we must look at its history.

The island's ancient name was Quizqueya; it was renamed La Isla Española by Columbus and its substantial population of Arawak people were eventually wiped out by new diseases brought in by the colonizers, forced labour and genocidal slaughter. Spanish entrepreneurs, who replaced the original inhabitants with African slaves at a rate of about 20,000 a year, changed its name to San Domingo. In 1697, following the Treaty of Rijswijk, the western third of the island was ceded by Spain to France. Under Spanish rule, sugar plantations worked by slave labour had been established in the coastal plains; subsequently, in 1734, coffee was planted in the mountainous foothills. San Domingo became Saint-Dominique and, rapidly, France's most valuable possession—it was among the richest colonies in the world. In 1791, the slaves, led by Toussaint L'Ouverture and inspired by the French Revolution, rebelled and, in 1804, created the world's first black republic. But it was not an entirely free republic—it could only survive by agreeing to pay exorbitant reparations to France and England. Above all, it was constantly harassed by US attempts at colonization.

Even though many of the actual plantations survived, the end of slavery brought with it the collapse of the plantation economy. In its place, an economy emerged which was unique in Latin America and largely based on peasant smallholdings. Much of the land was devoted to subsistence farming, but many farmers also grew coffee, indigo and cocoa. Such crops were sold cheaply to urban exporters who in turn sold them at enormous profits. A relatively small urban elite grew immensely rich on the trade while the farmers grew increasingly poor. The young state, controlled by the urban rich, largely depended on poor peasant taxpayers for its revenue. Since little of it was spent on rural welfare or investment, the smallholders and their dependants were doubly exploited. This exploitation led to the civil war of 1867 and the political instability and economic crises that followed it.

Haitian businessmen persuaded foreigners to invest in building infrastructure and in the purchase of sugar plantations. This led to the substantial repatriation of profits and, consequently, a highly unfavourable balance of payments deficit, chiefly with the US. By the end of the nineteenth century, a number of differing demands—commercial logging, charcoal burning to feed urban demand, industrialized sugar refining and rural wood fuel needs—increased the pressure on Haiti's forests. In 1915, Haiti failed to redeem its debts to US business and despite heroic resistance led initially by Charlemagne Péralte, the US invaded the island in November 1919. Péralte was assassinated by a US marine and the forces remained in occupation until 1934. Like most imperial powers, the occupiers spent their time extracting what they could from the conquered state and, in the process, increased the pressure on the forests by demanding wood, not only for export but also for further infrastructure to make extraction easier. They also took control of over 100,000 hectares of agricultural land, dispossessing thousands of peasants. Their greatest crime was the introduction of mass forced-labour overseen by the army—effectively, the reintroduction of slavery.

The US was finally persuaded to leave and its dependent Haitian elite began a long series of struggles for power that were characterized by constant coups and counter-coups and culminated in the notorious dictatorship, backed by the US, of 'Papa Doc' Duvalier. Swollen by the dispossessed, Haiti's capital, Port-au-Prince, became ever larger and its demands for wood fuel increased, leading to greater environmental destruction. Duvalier's rapacious regime eventually produced an armed reaction. Among the measures he took in his attempts to defeat it was to raze further substantial areas of a rapidly declining forest in the fond hope of denying cover to guerrillas. 'Papa Doc' died in 1971 and was succeeded by his equally viperous son, Jean-Claude, widely known as 'Baby Doc'.[21]

In the 1980s, when Haiti's population was around 6 million, 4.5 million peasants lived on holdings rarely measuring more that 1 hectare; it was estimated that 75 per cent of their land was severely degraded and most of them lived on the edge of starvation. Kleptocratic governments, backed by the US, remained in power but even they recognized that solutions to major problems had to be found. An unsurprising proposal entitled the 'American Plan' was instituted—a reaffirmation of free-market principles, it suggested that Haiti should trade on its strengths, the greatest of which was cheap labour. USAID promoted a substantial number of light industries, mainly assembly plants owned by US companies, in a scheme mimetic of Mexico's *maqiladora* factories.

In rural areas, US investment was principally devoted to farming for the export market. But, in 1986, the final collapse of the Duvaliers' ensanguined dictatorship made possible the sudden emergence of previously underground movements of 'peasants, slum dwellers, students and workers [who] saw the US approach as part of a plan to make Haiti economically dependent on its northern neighbour'.[22] Peasant movements in the villages began to organize cooperatives, credit systems and the recovery of land which had been either neglected or stolen. They introduced improved methods of crop storage and began re-aforestation and agro-forestry, soil preservation and land reform programmes.

In December 1990, a socially conscious Catholic priest, Jean-Baptiste Aristide, won the election as leader of the National Front for Change and Democracy. He was subsequently censured by his ecclesiastical superiors and expelled from his religious order for his interpretation of Liberation Theology—the ideology from which he drew his justification for the war against corruption and drug trafficking, the promotion of literacy and his campaign to uplift his people from abject poverty. He was deposed by a bloody military coup in September 1991. He left the country but, in 1994, was allowed to return. One of the conditions of his return, negotiated on Governor's Island in New York and brokered by the US, was that the Haitian government should enter into an agreement with the International Monetary Fund (IMF). A structural adjustment programme was to be installed in which any state-run enterprise would be privatized, import tariffs removed and, most importantly, exports would be promoted. This was clearly disastrous for the peasants, whose economic discourse ran entirely counter to the extractive and socially destructive policies of the IMF. Haiti could neither meet its debt repayments, nor return to profitability in the capitalist sense, unless it accepted the IMF shackles. Aristide's presidency lasted until 1996 but he was reinstated in 2001. In 2004, a dubious coup once again sent him into exile. The US backed the installation of the new prime minister, Gérard Latortue, and President Boniface Alexandre.

This brief history explains the circumstances in which the impoverished inhabitants of Haiti now have to cope with disaster—but it also points to the complicity in the creation of their difficulties of some of the states now offering assistance. Such offers invariably come with an agenda for what the donors regard as a rational route for the recovery and expansion of the economies of the afflicted country, and

Haiti is no exception. Many parallels may be seen elsewhere, particularly in the African continent—Third World poverty is a consequence of the rapacity of the developed world which in turn makes environmental disasters much worse. In essence, aid offered by wealthy states to poorer, and usually smaller, states comes with a price tag: the most common condition is the incorporation of the recipient state into the extractive norms of international capital.

The earthquake of 12 January 2010, the worst ever experienced in the region, led to appeals for humanitarian assistance by major relief institutions such as Oxfam which produced responses from around the world: funds, rescue teams, expert personnel and equipment were donated. But getting such assistance into Haiti was another matter. The earthquake had destroyed the country's communications systems—all transport, including that by sea, had been rendered inoperable and electricity supplies were seriously damaged. The road between Port-au-Prince in the north and Jacmel in the southern peninsula was blocked for 10 days after the earthquake. Rescue and aid efforts were, in consequence, seriously inhibited, not least because in that early stage no one knew who was in charge.

Another major difficulty was the disposal of many thousands of bodies—the morgues were unable to cope and the only solution was burial in mass graves. Much household accommodation was destroyed or badly damaged and many people took to sleeping in the streets, either because their living places were completely destroyed or because they were afraid that buildings still standing might collapse. Infrastructural difficulties, some of them a result of inadequate planning, led to considerable delays in the delivery of all kinds of assistance.

They resulted in some looting and occasional violence but also raised the ire of both aid workers and survivors. Another consequence was a substantial exodus of refugees to the Dominican Republic which responded by insisting that only those in need of medical attention could stay and only for as long as their treatment lasted. A Dominican provincial governor pointed out that the Republic's own stocks of food and medical necessities were limited.

By 22 January, 10 days after this massive event, the UN was able to announce the end of the emergency phase of international assistance. But the long-term ramifications remained—one of considerable importance was the major damage done to the clothing industry, which collectively had accounted for about two-thirds of Haiti's exports. More immediately, the organization of relief and the control of the airport were taken over by the US military, an organization not noted for its expertise in disaster relief. Armies are not designed for humanitarianism and have little competence in dealing with such disasters; what they can do sometimes, where they already have a presence in or near the natural disaster, is to give immediate logistical help or, in some cases, protection. Even so, their deployment should be under the aegis of the UN. One result of their control in Haiti was the diversion of relief supplies from states other than the US to the Dominican Republic with consequent delays in delivery and additional expense in cost, to say nothing of the international diplomatic squabble it created. Crass mistakes were common—a particularly egregious example was seen in the delivery of emergency food aid that came in concentrated or powdered form. Instructions for its use were in English, a language not spoken by most of Haiti's population and the recipients had no idea what to do with it.

Six weeks after the earthquake, when some semblance of coordination should have been apparent, rescue organizations were still acting as if it were an emergency. One possible cause for the muddle seems to have been an inexplicably bureaucratic approach to the organization of emergency aid. For instance, one report said it took a Haitian official three days to get his community recognized by the World Food Programme's administration.[23] Causes are unclear, but it is at least probable that the confusion and ineptitude were by-products of the US insistence that matters should be left in the hands of the US Army rather than being handed over to organizations already in the field who were experienced in such disasters. Such insistence suggests that the US, like the UK in similar circumstances, finds it difficult to abandon its colonizing habit of mind. As in so many disasters, what was overlooked was the resilience and ability of the Haitian people; while assistance in kind and medical reinforcement are necessary, people are more capable of managing their own affairs than they are given credit for.

SOMALIA: CHRONIC DISASTER AND THE ANARCHY OF AID

Somalian independence from its former colonizers was declared on 1 July 1960 and its two colonized regions were united in the new Republic of Somalia. As in most of the world, it included both secular and religious factions as well as social and economic differences between rural and urban communities. Another social disconnection was that between those with nationwide aspirations and others clinging to sectarian ambitions. Other differences, for example between pastoralists and settled farmers, were less universal but still widespread. Independence brought about an extraordinary national unity and sense of patriotism—to most people all things seemed possible and these differences, none of them peculiar to Somalia, were certainly not thought to be insurmountable.

In the post-Second World War process of decolonization, independence was rarely succeeded by *tabulae rasae*. At best, new governments were formed by the most powerful elements in the battles for emancipation, not necessarily by those most dedicated to new and all-encompassing democracies. In the case of Somalia, British colonialism had left another hostage to fortune in its early ceding of the Ogaden province, ethnically a largely Somali region, to Ethiopia. Euphoric patriotism in 1964 led to substantial Somali support for an attempt at recovering the province by force. It failed, and the consequences have rumbled on ever since. But that year was important for another reason—an unelected but popular interim government, dominated by the Somali Youth League, a major northern party, had taken power at independence. A large part of its remit was to enable free parliamentary elections, an event which also took place in 1964. Much of the interim government was re-elected but, apart from a desire to ensure that the country should develop, it became clear that it had neither interest in, nor understanding of, the popular openness to a united secular state.

President Aden Abdulle Osman and Prime Minister Abdirazak Haji Hussein did what they could to bring north and south (the two former colonies) together, but failed to make this agenda apparent. It was also clear that the residual bureaucracy, following decolonization, was woefully unequal to the task of administering an independent state. In the presidential elections of 1967, Osman was ousted and replaced by Abdirashid Ali Sharmarke, who appointed Abdirahman Ahmed Ali as prime minister in place of Hussein. Osman and Hussein had run a strong anti-corruption campaign—unlike Sharmarke who had promised to reward the members of parliament who gave him their votes. Corruption, sectarianism and misgovernment prevailed until 1969 when the military, led by Siad Barre, intervened.

The coup gained almost immediate popular support—the junta ended corrupt government, halted the progress of sectarianism and was effective in dealing with the drought of 1973–74. It introduced the Latin script for the Somali language and broadened access to education. But it was assisted financially by the Soviet Union and made ill-judged and inept attempts at reproducing Soviet supply-side economic management. In 1977–78, it launched another minor war aimed at recovering Ogaden and its defeat, combined with dissent from the public and from sections of the military, led to a collapse into oppressive government. A form of what Abdi Samatar has called 'collective paranoia' led to massive military attacks on large regions of the country suspected by the junta of harbouring dissidents; in 1988, government forces razed the northern cities of Hargeisa and Burao.[24]

A number of guerrilla opposition groups emerged, the most important of which were associated with the Somali National Movement funded by Ethiopia. They were effective, but what determined the defeat of the junta was the end of the cold war.

From 1989, aid provided by various 'cold warriors' largely came to an end and, in January 1991, the regime collapsed. But factionalism, opportunism and the scale of the damage produced by the internecine war that followed resulted in the complete collapse of any functioning state. In May 1991, four months after the collapse of the Barre regime, the Somali National Movement established the secessionist state of 'Somaliland' in the north-west of the country. Roughly coterminous with the former British Somaliland, it has never been recognized as a legitimate state. Despite a rocky beginning, it brought peace of a kind and allowed the arrival of international humanitarian intervention which facilitated some infrastructural recovery. Matters had improved to the point where the International Crisis Group could describe the regime as 'a functioning constitutional democracy'.[25] The George Bush Sr regime (1989–93) provided substantial training for officers in Somaliland's army, but the world at large—including the UN, major aid donors and INGOs—continued to see the infant republic only as part of a country affected by an acute and complex emergency. An elaborate dance was performed around the non-existent Somaliland whose cooperation was needed for access to people in need elsewhere in Somalia. Few humanitarian agencies operated anywhere in Somalia at the time of the collapse of the state and although some small forms of assistance were evident, mainly in Mogadishu and Kismayo, intervention became possible only after the interim but largely powerless President Ali Mahdi and the principal warlord, General Mohammed Farah Aideed, agreed to a ceasefire. It was an unstable agreement but sufficient for the UN to act.

The first UN operation in Somalia was launched in April 1992 and became known as UNOSOM 1. It was designed to monitor the ceasefire and to secure the deliveries of humanitarian supplies for Mogadishu and its environs; in July 1992, it was extended to Berbera and Bossasso.[26] Almost immediately, it encountered pressure from several of the warring factions to conform to their agendas, and was unquestionably hampered by the common failure of donor states to provide the funds they had promised.[27] By December 1992, the situation had deteriorated to the point where a large military force, designed to contain the problems, was seen by the UN as the only solution. This proposition was supported by the US only on the condition that US forces should lead the expedition. The UN–US despatched UNITAF, a taskforce of 40,000 mainly US troops, which, in a moment of absurd hubris, the US called 'Operation Restore Hope'. Its mission was to negotiate peace between the warlords and to secure humanitarian assistance for people afflicted by massive displacement and famine. Those objectives were rapidly abandoned and the nest was further fouled by the Operation's pursuit of just one warlord, Aideed. This idiocy was compounded by inadequate planning and unclear objectives, both of which led to the forces becoming involved in the factional fighting. They were eventually compelled to beat a retreat in 1994.

The Gulf of Aden has long been strategically important and remained so after the collapse of the Soviet Union and the consequent realignment of international relations throughout the Middle East, Arabia and the Greater Horn of Africa. The international response to the catastrophe in Somalia was another indication of its importance, but such responses are not confined to delivering relief supplies, particularly when emergencies remain acute. Quite apart from the compromises necessary to ensure access to the people who are suffering—compromises which inevitably modify the politics—the Wilsonian imperative demands that donor states also attempt to facilitate the re-establishment of a working government, or, where one exists, the creation of circumstances which allow it to rule. It is this endeavour that helped to produce the precarious situation following the 'humanitarian' attempt to create and install a provisional government in Somalia.

In 2004, when the negotiations surrounding the creation of that government were at an advanced stage, I was employed in an evaluation of the Netherlands' humanitarian assistance to Somalia. That assistance, like all other international activity in the country, was administered from Nairobi; enquiries among the many relevant authorities and organizations showed that virtually all of them had a map of Somalia on their walls in which the country was divided into clan 'territories'. The common assumption was that if boundaries could be agreed, then the ancient clan relationships could be restored and a basis for peace be created. This solution was the preferred position of the US and was casually taken for granted by many others, including many UN agencies, implementing organizations and some embassies. Quite apart from the failure of those who adopted this analysis to understand either the clan system or its origins in nomadic pastoralism, they also failed to realize that family and livelihoods are of far greater overall importance, and that for pastoralists concepts of territory and borders are completely alien.

Imposing settled and urban concepts on a pastoralist society both played into the hands of local warlords and other builders of petty fiefdoms, and ensured the defeat of modernizing and secular ambitions. It led, finally, to the creation of a crippled provisional government largely made up of erstwhile warlords. This dubious entity, hailed by many aid donors as a triumph of democracy, began its fractious existence in Nairobi and, when it finally got to Somalia, was more or less confined to the town of Baidoa. But the people of Mogadishu and its surrounding territories imposed their own solution in the form of the Union of Islamic Courts. The Union had made encouraging noises about replacing shari'a with secular courts as soon as possible and about upholding human rights. Membership of the Union certainly included people in favour of secular democracy. But in December 2006, the Union was defeated by a coalition of the warlords and Ethiopia, the latter backed by the US, which declared the Union to be a terrorist organization.

Since the fall of Siad Barre, most foreign interventions in Somalia have been defined as humanitarian assistance. The Netherlands and the Scandinavian countries are usually thought to be the most disinterested of donors and the most likely to work towards freeing the afflicted from outside interference. All of them made donations towards the cost of saving lives in the acute stages of the Somali emergency and, to a considerable degree, such intervention is a form of first aid, no matter how frequently it has to be given. When such crises move to their 'chronic' phase—when the fighting has largely subsided and continues only sporadically but there is neither viable governmental control of public services nor any effective government—then the givers of aid expand their activities to fill that absence. A close examination of, for example, Dutch assistance makes clear that it was directed towards establishing the conditions necessary for government. Aid went well beyond fundamental humanitarian objectives—the provision of food, water, medical care, shelter and protection—to include support not only for the organizing mechanisms of these elements (production, hospitals and clinics, housing) but also for building schools and infrastructure for third-level education, training and a host of proto-developmental initiatives. All this may be laudable, but it is also profoundly political—it could hardly be anything else. But, since politics cannot be neutral, the questions about the long-term aims of such intervention are obvious. The Netherlands, as all other European donors along with the US, turned a blind eye to the vicious constituent elements of the would-be Somali government-in-Nairobi and supported it, possibly in the dubious conviction that almost any 'stable' government was better than none.

The Bush administration and its Ethiopian ally, both of them obliquely supported by the European determination to back the Transitional Federal Government, have, in the name of humanitarian assistance, created today's mess in which anarchy and piracy confirm the destruction of

Somalia. To some extent, the UN and a variety of NGOs have contrived to deliver food, medical care and protection in an uncertain and necessarily unplanned campaign. Personnel can only work in 'safe' areas and such places are constantly under threat from a variety of violent forces; aid workers of all kinds are frequently driven from their centres of action. Although European humanitarian assistance unquestionably made a difference to the lives of many besieged people, its application, methods and limits were determined by European and US accounts of suitable structures of Somali governance.

Despite becoming an instrument of US' Middle-East policy, the 1992 debacle was launched under the colours of an international humanitarian intervention. Bush's post-9/11 demonizing of Islam and his support for the invasion of Somalia by Ethiopia in December 2006 has led to a continuous onslaught on Somalia. The US launched bombing attacks in southern Somalia in 2007–08 to kill people the Bush regime had described as linked to al-Qaeda or to some other enemy of the US. The bombs missed most of their intended targets but did kill a number of civilians. In its campaign against what it sees as its Islamic enemies, the US has trained a number of Somali military officers, an activity that defies the UN's Somalia Arms Embargo Monitoring Group. At the time of writing, the US was preparing for another attack, this time on the extreme Islamic group, al-Shabab, considered al-Qaeda's proxy in the failed Horn of Africa state.

SUDAN: THE HIGH PRICE OF OIL

The catastrophe of colonization overtook the entire continent of Africa. Differences in its effects arose from differing African civilizations and, above all, differing covetable resources. Any account of contemporary issues must keep in mind the continuing effects of that history, not least because of the kinds of government which emerged from the slow collapse of direct colonization and the emergence, in its place, of colonizing financial and resource development, which became known as neo-colonialism. European and North American meddling has encouraged a substantial series of corrupt and often tyrannical governments; lately China, particularly in Sudan and Kenya, has joined in this unsavoury mix of political engineering and resource-grubbing.

In the case of Sudan, Egyptian interest either in controlling the country or in securing close relationships with it also has a long history. The Anglo-Egyptian Condominium, which ruled Sudan prior to independence, was created following separate colonizing adventures by Egypt, France and Britain. French forces were compelled to withdraw, leaving Britain and Egypt, who recognized that collaboration over the management of the Nile basin was preferable to a pointless war. The Second World War brought about a brief interregnum, but the Condominium was subsequently re-established and lasted until Sudan's declaration of independence on 1 January 1956.[28] Since then, Sudan has been ruled, with occasional exceptions, by a series of oligarchies; since1989, rule has been in the hands of a coterie headed by General Omar Hassan al-Bashir. Following independence, Egyptian interference in Sudan, occasionally erupting into low-level but violent hostilities, has been common and is a result of Egypt's anxiety about the Nile. The conflicts continue and it is at least possible that they will escalate substantially as climate change increases.

Public awareness that a terrible war is being fought in Darfur is extensive, but it is also notoriously misinformed and much of that misinformation is a consequence of international political agendas. It is necessary to remind ourselves that it is not a war between Arabs and Black Africans—Gérard Prunier has described the varied use of the term 'Arab' which, in Darfur and much of the South, is a cultural rather than an ethnic description and is used differently depending on the region, ethnicity and occupation of the user.[29] One of the consequences of an unparalleled series of Sahelian droughts has been growing tension between nomadic pastoralists and settled farmers as they both fight for the same resources. In the past, competition for both land and water was usually settled by negotiation and only occasionally by fighting. The drought reversed the order and violent conflict became the norm.

The drought was not the only cause: in Darfur, the infamous Janjaweed—which largely replaced conventional forces and acted as Khartoum's frontline force, backed up by relatively small numbers of soldiers from the regular forces—also did its utmost to promote violence in the interests of the central government. It is these interests that we have to consider and there are two elements to them: the history of the relationship between Darfur and Khartoum, and oil. Darfur was incorporated into Sudan in 1916 by the Anglo-Egyptian Condominium but, once that had been achieved, the region—about the size of France and very remote—was completely ignored by the central powers. Following Sudan's independence, that neglect continued. Responses in Darfur became increasingly militant and were, in turn, met with violent repression by Khartoum.

Current problems in Chad—where a 35-year-long intermittent civil war between Muslim pastoralist and largely Christian farmers continues to divide the country—are inextricably linked to those in Darfur. Confusion in Chad was mirrored in Darfur. Farmers and pastoralists have always competed for land and water, but the lengthening periods of Sahelian drought had led to the collapse of negotiation and to violent skirmishes. Khartoum, opposed to the ambitions of the Sudan Liberation Movement, and aware that oil was to be found at least in the state of Southern Darfur and possibly in Western Darfur, used the deteriorating situation to drive the militant opposition and the people from the land. In 2003, Khartoum launched its attacks on the region, both by air and by the use of the Janjaweed. Large numbers of people were slaughtered, and tens of thousands more of all ethnicities in the region were driven into internal displacement within Sudan or as refugees into Chad. Most of the consequences are well known, but what is less commonly discussed is the effect of this movement of people on the overall situation between the two countries.

Early April 2007 provided an example of activity which had been commonplace for much of the preceding four years—the Janjaweed attacked two villages in Chad, Tiero and Marena, killing 65 people and wounding another 70. The UNHCR reported that 'between 2,000 and 3,000' more people had sought refuge in its Goz Amir refugee camp, which was already sheltering over 19,000 refugees from Sudan; the UN also reported that '140,000 displaced Chadians and 235,000 Sudanese refugees are now sheltering in the barren eastern deserts'. They were supported as far as possible by the UN and NGOs, but support is inhibited by continuous fighting. All this happened only two months after the Chadian President Idriss Déby and al-Bashir had signed a peace agreement. Since then, matters have become yet more catastrophic—the United Nations Office for the Coordination of Humanitarian Affairs' (UNOCHA) mid-year revue in July 2008 reported that a further 200,000 people were displaced, bringing the total to 4.3 million. At the time of writing, heavy fighting over the control of oil had also broken out around Abyei in central south Sudan between Sudanese government forces and a variety of regional factions.

Sudan's southern war, together with what is, in effect, its civil war in Darfur, its intermittent battles with Chad and the growing tensions in the east of the country are all constituents in a steadily worsening complex humanitarian disaster. At its centre is a tyrannical government and the increasingly important issue of oil converging in the not-unfamiliar spectacle of oligarchic rapacity. Additional elements in the disaster have included mischievous meddling by

Bush and his oil industry employers, Chinese determination to secure oil supplies and differing objectives among the EU nations who contribute to humanitarian assistance. Assistance provided by the US has the dubious advantage of being unashamedly part of its foreign policy for the area, which is largely devoted to securing its own oil supplies. China's assistance, also motivated by its interest in Sudanese oil, is devoted to developmental ends and is largely dictated by the agenda of the Khartoum government.

Humanitarian assistance in complex disasters is always sporadic; no matter how devoted and courageous humanitarian workers (many of them indigenous volunteers) may be, they are frequently unable to operate when extensive violence erupts. The catastrophe in Darfur was particularly difficult. Tensions between settled farmers and nomadic pastoralists were acute and competition for water and fodder had become increasingly violent. Khartoum's neglect of the region had led to increasingly well-organized opposition, which the Sudanese government determined to destroy rather than meet its legitimate demands. In the period 2003–05, most donors had their eyes firmly fixed on the resolution of the conflict between Khartoum and South Sudan and completely failed to respond adequately to the growing crisis in Darfur. For varied reasons, initial responses were paltry and slow to emerge—supplies of all kinds had to be transported from Port Sudan to the region, a journey of about 1,500 km; the personnel available were few in number and not always sufficiently equipped; and the ravages of the Janjaweed ensured an unmanageable stream of destitute and terrified refugees. Many other factors were also at play, including the intransigence of the Khartoum government, meddling by

Libya, the complexity of relations with Chad—many of the people of Eastern Chad are 'Fur', as are the majority in Darfur, literally 'the country of the Fur'—and international as well as national interest in what may well be significant deposits of oil.[30] The overall result is a number of volatile catastrophes in which humanitarian assistance is often a dangerous business and a profoundly political one.

WHAT IS TO BE DONE?

My assertion that humanitarian assistance is a central element in foreign policy is scarcely new—most 'humanitarians' regard it as the necessary price to be paid for bringing help to people in dire straits. Each arena of action is discrete, the needs to be met commonly exceed the available human and material resources and the work is constant and demanding. In many cases the active presence of UN personnel and equipment and, in some instances, neutral military forces promotes the impression that an intervention is supranational and disinterested and not the fragile underfunded entity that it actually is. Nonetheless, lives are saved and, following the immediate crisis, some reconstruction becomes possible. It is, therefore, unsurprising that while most expatriate humanitarian workers are aware of the national origins of much of their funding and of the role of foreign ministries in it, they do not connect the origins and political rhetoric of that funding with, for example, the destruction of Iraq, Afghanistan and Somalia, where military campaigns also march under the banner of humanitarian assistance.

The rhetoric of humanitarianism frequently includes assertions of the right to assistance for people who are *in extremis* but, as Joana Abrisketa has pointed out, 'The legality of humanitarian action is not clearly defined in International Law' and, inserted into the Geneva Conventions and Protocols, there is a defence of the principle of state sovereignty—humanitarian action is only permissible if the government of the state at issue agrees to it.[31] In the case of failed states, humanitarian assistance, even if sanctioned by the UN, is usually accompanied by unseemly manoeuvring by the donating powers to persuade compliant elements in the failed state to form an interim government; Somalia, Afghanistan, Liberia and, to a considerable degree, Bosnia are all examples. Such governments are almost invariably designed to neutralize warring parties and to conform to the external powers' perceptions of what is politically desirable.

An important question is whether or not people in extremis really do have a right to humanitarian assistance. The Geneva Conventions and Protocols assert that right for the afflicted, but a measure of uncertainty in its exercise is introduced by the condition that such assistance must be agreed with the government of the country in which it is to be offered—a provision which plainly casts doubt on whether it can be a human right at all. In the case of failed states, there is a loose supposition that the UN must authorize any action. For a right to be anything other than a moral exhortation, it must be justiciable and, up to a limited point, the International Criminal Court (ICC) is the arena for this; but since the US refuses to allow any of its citizens to be tried by it, no matter how serious the charges may be, the limits are considerable. Eric Hobsbawm makes the point succinctly: 'Even when world courts are established by general agreement [. . .] their judgements will not necessarily be accepted as legitimate and binding, so long as powerful states are in a position to disregard them.'[32]

From its inception, the US–UK-led invasion of Iraq could only be justified by what is now a well-recognized barrage of lies. Wilsonian claims that the invasion was a humanitarian intervention aside, this well-known history illustrates the fragility of the ICC. The framework for the justiciability of rights exists but, as long as it is rejected or ignored by most of the world's major powers, it means little. Rights in general are not justiciable unless the Court is respected and, in the absence of that respect, they continue to be aspirations or proposals. Any 'right' to humanitarian assistance is also weakened both by the Geneva Convention's caveat and by the neutering of the ICC. A rights agenda which is not sanctioned and governed by international law and justice is often used in rhetoric justifying war—the devastation of Iraq and the slaughter of so many of its people is the result of a war described by its perpetrators as a defence of Iraqis' human rights against the tyranny of Saddam Hussein. Guantánamo Bay and torture centres around the world exist to defend the rights of 'citizens' to live in peace.

Ambiguity lies at the heart of this analysis—not all assistance is cover for asset grabbing, even when it forms an integral part of each donor nation's foreign policies. Despite the malignant role of the Security Council, the only organizations with some capacity to transcend the maze of individual foreign policy objectives are the UN and, in a smaller way, the Red Cross/Red Crescent group. Humanitarian assistance is politically directed by nations committed to the ascendancy of capital's project of global control, and many complex disasters are direct or indirec, consequences of that project. The extractive nature of globalization and its tendency to rapidly increase poverty, despite its claims, have been well documented.[33] If we exclude the more grotesque claims that Western 'humanitarian' intervention is an errand of mercy, as in the cases of Iraq, Afghanistan, Somalia, as well as in earlier instances such as Vietnam, then the overall situation can be seen as a very complex one—lives are saved and some situations are improved even though those situations tend towards the support of the wealthy world's political and economic intentions. But we are left with the greatest of all aporias: to what can we turn for an alternative form of humanitarian assistance?

Current complex emergencies are principally the product of capital's need to perpetually accumulate and thus inevitably to exclude populations of no further economic importance. It is a process which reaches its apogee in the equally worldwide degradation of the environment evinced in climate change. Once again, those who played the smallest part, if any, in its creation are, and will continue to be, its main victims. The imposition on them of what Giorgio Agamben, in his book *Homo Sacer* (1998), calls 'the state of exception'—for example, the misleadingly named 'asylum process'—may be seen in the increasing paranoia of the governments of Europe. The indigent and imperilled need not apply for help but, since they are reduced to *homines sacri*, should they do so they will be returned to their lethal origins. *Homo sacer* is guilty until proved innocent and causing his or her death is not a crime.[34]

In any consideration of the question of humanitarian assistance we have to remember that, with the exception of the Red Cross/Red Crescent group, the voluntary sector is compromised by its dependence on national organizational and governmental support.[35] The difficulty is encapsulated in the description of voluntary groups as 'non-governmental organizations', including those with the prefix 'international'; they are thus defined in relation to governments, which in turn both support and regulate them. In practice, they may criticise their governments but may not actively campaign against them. This means that although the front-line staff of NGOs work heroically and often very effectively, they may do so only within the remit of their governments' foreign policies and only in regions or countries sanctioned by their own governments or those of closely allied states. A second problem arises from the NGO structure. Each organization is dependent on state funding and on public donations; both are competitive and while competition may lead to the improvement of practical standards, it seriously inhibits coordination, central to all humanitarian assistance. Some governments make half-hearted attempts at wider regulation; the UK, for example, decided some years ago that governmental funds for INGOs should go to a relatively small number of them who would, in turn, be charged with employing applicant organizations as subcontractors for the aims at issue. A strong argument may be made for the consequent reduction of administrative expenditure and for the regulation of standards, but the system also reinforces the regulation of objectives and their compliance with foreign policy.

What we have now to consider is the most central, and in some ways the most crippled, of all international bodies—the United Nations. It was born shackled by the imposition of the Security Council in which most countries have only a limited and rotational presence. The five states holding permanent seats on the Security Council do so as a consequence of the political landscape following the Second World War, and the voting structure gives them extraordinary power. The Security Council deals only with what are termed 'substantive' issues—matters which are not procedural, and all 15 members have a vote on any such matters as come before it. But the five permanent members have a veto. It is a malign device, not only because it is frequently used solely in the interests of the foreign policies of the state wielding it, but also because it weakens the General Assembly. If resolutions on matters of substance are to get through the Security Council, then they must be constructed in ways that will not attract a veto. Until some reform is accomplished, the UN as a whole is compromised and, despite the often heroic work of some of its agencies, will always fall short of its principal targets, particularly in its work in humanitarian assistance.

Nonetheless, it remains that the UN and the Red Cross family are the only supranational entities able to act without direct reference to national foreign policies, even though both may be constrained by them and have to work within their effects.

The role of UN agencies in humanitarian assistance is crucial in more ways than one. So long as funds are available, they have degrees of ability and flexibility unrivalled except by imperial armies. Since, in theory at least, the UN and its agencies are not partisan, they are more readily acceptable to the frequently precarious states in which they must operate—even the violent and felonious government of Sudan finds itself forced into appearing to accommodate UN intervention in its onslaught on Darfur. If humanitarian assistance is to be prised loose of the constraints normally attached to it by donating states, then it must in all instances be under the control of, and not just an addition to, UN agencies and, in certain circumstances, the Red Cross/Red Crescent group. But there is a difficulty. The UN, despite the antics of the Security Council, is seen throughout the world as a possible forum where some universal standards of justice can be secured. Hence the major powers seek to control it and to undermine its independence, but not to destroy it. The UN remains a necessary instrument in international exchange, law and diplomacy and is the only organization with the managerial and organizational capacity to deal simultaneously with a number of complex and chronic disasters.

There are other obvious reasons why humanitarian assistance should be recognized as the responsibility of the UN. I have already pointed to the close links between national foreign policy objectives and unilateral aid and, while such objectives might also be furthered by donations to multi-lateral assistance through the UN, they can be superseded to a considerable degree. This may be seen in the increasing role of UN-OCHA, particularly in its oversight of NGO activity. A large proportion of the personnel active in humanitarian relief is provided by NGOs which also attract significant public funding. Those involved in international humanitarian assistance or development, come in three principal forms. The largest organizations, such as Oxfam, do have a presence in the fields of activity but are more heavily and effectively engaged in fundraising, research and campaigning (the latter is usually known in the language of the movements as 'advocacy' and includes pressing governments into greater responses). Oxfam commonly employs or finances smaller or specialist NGOs for what is called the 'delivery' of aid. A second major group is that of organizations dedicated to particular kinds of work, of which Médecins Sans Frontières is a good example. The third—if it can be thought of as a group—is the myriad smaller organizations, some general and others specialist, to whom specific tasks are allotted either by governments or by the large intermediary NGOs. There are now so many of them that most donating governments have resorted to some sort of filter. In the UK, for example, it consists of the shortlist of major NGOs with which the government will deal and which have, in effect, become contractors. Another instance of this filtering is in the Netherlands where an independent intermediary body performs the same task.

A further major and continuing job for the UN in any emergency is in coordinating aid. Any failure to do so results, among many other evils, in wasted resources, in failures to reach many of the most vulnerable people, particularly those in remote and difficult circumstances, and in pointless duplication. Yet it is an activity often resented by NGOs as a curb on the exercise of their skills and resources. Coordination is so essential to contemporary emergencies, particularly those classified as complex, that

UNOCHA—once a small support agency—has become the UN's principal agency for administration and, to a considerable degree, its policy instrument in all disasters.

UNOCHA's humanitarian activities are not exempt from the damage that the Security Council can inflict—essential humanitarian assistance can be forbidden, as is the case among others of the US veto of even the very modest assistance for Palestine. UN intervention can also be compromised, as in the farcical episode in Somalia in 1992–93. But since organization and policy cannot entirely be separated, the UN's independence in humanitarian activity from the dominant imperial, or would-be imperial, powers is increasing.

Finally, public recognition of the centrality of the UN to all humanitarian assistance is vitally important. Public engagement provides the only hope of pushing governments into curbing the predatory habits of the permanent members of the Security Council and of reducing their control of the organization. While humanitarian assistance is dominated by the Wilsonian recognition that it is necessarily political, what is required of an interested public is that it should do its utmost to compel its parliaments into far more impartial responses to disaster than is commonly the case.

Notes

1 Two other categories are sometimes used: technological catastrophes, of which Bhopal is probably the most infamous example, and industrial catastrophes, of which the only too probable disaster of climate change may become the prime example.

2 For example, China is the largest customer for Sudanese oil and has invested heavily in improving infrastruc-

ture often at the cost of substantial forced displacement of indigenous populations.

3 Phillip Inman and Ian Cobain, 'Development Fund "Uses Private Equity-type Policies"', *The Guardian,* 10 November 2008.

4 For a similar comment see Mahmood Mamdani, 'The Politics of Naming: Genocide, Civil War, Insurgency', in *The London Review of Books* 29(5) (March 2007).

5 Woodrow Wilson's 'Fourteen Points' were contained in a speech delivered to a joint session of the US Congress on 8 January 1918, which set out the broad framework of US foreign policy following the end of the First World War.

6 In 1949, a variety of subsequent conventions were pulled together to form the existing body. Convention II extended the first Convention to cover those wounded at sea; Convention III refers to the treatment of prisoners of war; Convention IV extends protection to

civilians in time of war. Protocol I extends protection to victims of wars against racist regimes and wars of self-determination; Protocol II covers protection of those affected by internal conflict.

7 Ilan Pappe, *The Ethnic Cleansing of Palestine* (Oxford: One World Publications, 2006), p. 203.

8 Clive Stafford Smith, *Bad Men*: *Guantánamo Bay and the Secret Prisons* (London: Weidenfeld and Nicolson, 2007), p. 14.

9 Eduardo Galeano, *Open Veins of Latin America*: *Five Centuries of the Pillage of a Continent* (New York: Monthly Review Press, 1997), p. 107.

10 Galeano, *Open Veins of Latin America*.

11 It may be of passing interest that this war against the people of the Philippines was conducted under the command of one General Douglas MacArthur, father to his eponymous son who led the post-Second World War US occupation of the archipelago.

12 Ruth First made this point some decades ago and in her book *The Barrel of a Gun*:

Political power in Africa and the Coup d'État (London: Allen Lane, 1970), which provides an analytical catalogue (she called it 'A Coup Inventory') of military interventions. See pp. 205–21.

13 See www.whitehouse.gov

14 In May 2005, General Sutarto, with the help of US forces, killed 3,000 'rebels' in Aceh. His record in Indonesia itself and in East Timor (where he was responsible for Indonesian strategy) is unrelievedly bloody.

15 Brian Barry, *Justice as Impartiality: A Treatise on Social Justice*, VOL. II (Oxford: Clarendon Press, 1995), pp. 13–27.

16 Ibid., p. 17.

17 Ibid., p. 27.

18 There are a few honourable exceptions. Some NGOs do publish analyses which attack the corporate rape of the Third World. Examples may be seen in, inter alia, two pamphlets written by Dominic Eagleton for ActionAid International: 'Power Hungry: Six Reasons to Regulate Global Food Companies' [available at

http://actionaid.org.uk/index.asp?page_id=100222], 1 January 2005; and 'Under the Influence: Exposing Undue Corporate Influence over Policy-making at the WTO' [available at http://actionaid.org.uk/index.asp?page_id=100222], 25 January 2006.

19 Patrick Bond, *Looting Africa: the Economics of Exploitation* (Pietmarizburg: University of KwaZulu-Natal Press and London: Zed Books, 2006), p. 21.

20 1976 (13 dead and 40,000 homeless); 1980 (2,735 dead and 1,500 missing); 1997 (13 dead and 40,000 homeless).

21 It is estimated that his regime was responsible for 40,000 murders—his principal instruments in this carnage were the infamous Tonton Macoutes.

22 Arthur Charles, 'Confronting Haiti's Environmental Crisis: A Tale of Two Visions', in Helen Collinson (ed.), *Green Guerrillas: Environmental Conflicts and Initiatives in Latin America and the Caribbean* (London: Latin American Bureau, 1996), pp. 149–57.

23 See www.haitianalysis.com.

24 Professor Abdi Samatar, a Somali, holds a chair in geography in the University of Minnesota.

25 International Crisis Group, 'Somaliland: Time for African Union Leadership' (Africa Report No. 110) [available at www.crisisgroup.org/en/regions/africa/-horn-of-africa/somalia/110-somaliland-time-for-african-union-leadership.aspx], 23 May 2006.

26 See www.un.org/Depts/DPKO/Missions/-unosomi.htm

27 Donors had pledged US$82.7 million for the UN's 100-Day Programme for Accelerated Humanitarian Assistance, but it received only US$67.3 million.

28 Basil Davidson, *Modern Africa: A Social and Political History* (New York: Longman, 1994), pp. 110–12.

29 Gérard Prunier, *Darfur: The Ambiguous Genocide* (Ithaca: Cornell University Press, 2005), pp. 4–6. See also Neil Middleton and Phil O'Keefe, 'Politics, History and Problems of Humanitarian

Assistance in Sudan', in *Review of African Political Economy* 33(109) (September 2006): 543–59.

30 'Darfur' means 'the land of the Fur'; see Prunier, pp. 5–6.

31 Joana Abrisketa, 'The Right to Humanitarian Aid: Basis and Limitations', in Humanitarian Studies Unit, the Transnational Institute (ed.), *Reflections on Humanitarian Action: Principles, Ethics, and Contradictions* (London: Pluto Press, 2001), p. 55.

32 Eric Hobsbawm, *Globalisation, Democracy and Terrorism* (London: Little Brown, 2007), p. 24.

33 See, *inter alia*, Bond, *Looting Africa*.

34 Giorgio Agamben, *Homo Sacer: Sovereign Power and Bare Life* (Stanford: Stanford University Press, 1998).

35 Neither the International Committee of the Red Cross (ICRC) nor the IFRC can really be described as part of the 'voluntary sector', but although they are not NGOs and are collectively *sui generis*,

they are commonly seen as such by the public.